PEACE

on EARTH BEGINS

with YOU

Also by Faridi McFree

CELEBRATE YOU:
SELF-HEALING THROUGH ART AND AFFIRMATIONS

PEACE

ON EARTH BEGINS

WITH YOU

Simple Steps Each of Us Can Take
to Bring Harmony to Our World

· FARIDI McFREE ·

EAGLE BROOK   WILLIAM MORROW AND COMPANY, INC.   NEW YORK

PUBLISHED BY EAGLE BROOK
AN IMPRINT OF WILLIAM MORROW AND COMPANY, INC.
1350 AVENUE OF THE AMERICAS, NEW YORK, N.Y. 10019

IT IS THE POLICY OF WILLIAM MORROW AND COMPANY, INC., AND
ITS IMPRINTS AND AFFILIATES, RECOGNIZING THE IMPORTANCE
OF PRESERVING WHAT HAS BEEN WRITTEN, TO PRINT THE BOOKS
WE PUBLISH ON ACID-FREE PAPER, AND WE EXERT OUR BEST
EFFORTS TO THAT END.

LIBRARY OF CONGRESS CATALOGING-IN-PUBLICATION DATA

MCFREE, FARIDI.
    PEACE ON EARTH BEGINS WITH YOU : SIMPLE STEPS EACH
  OF US CAN TAKE TO BRING HARMONY TO OUR WORLD / FARIDI
  MCFREE.—1ST ED.
      P.   CM.
    ISBN 0-688-15651-7 (ALK. PAPER)
    1. CONDUCT OF LIFE. 2. PEACE OF MIND. 3. PEACE.
  I. TITLE.
  BJ1595.M44   1997
  170'.44—DC21   97-22827
                                                      CIP

PRINTED IN THE UNITED STATES OF AMERICA

FIRST EDITION

1 2 3 4 5 6 7 8 9 10

BOOK DESIGN BY LEAH S. CARLSON

WWW.WILLIAMMORROW.COM

$\mathcal{I}$N THE SPIRIT OF PEACE

AND

GROWING TOGETHER

IN

HARMONY WITH THE UNIVERSE

A Royal Dedication

As founder of the Studio of the Healing Hearts and a trustee of the Metropolitan Peace Museum, we would like to celebrate Princess Diana's noble work in her efforts to bring about a more peaceful and more humane world, especially her work for the world's children and the victims of the weapons of war.

Let us remember the Queen of Hearts by allowing her royal seeds of peace to grow and flourish. Make her fairy tale come true. Let Peace on Earth Begin with You!

Faridi McFree

Acknowledgments

MY DEEPEST APPRECIATION TO A VERY UNUSUAL
AND SPECIAL TALENT AGENT. . . .
MR. NAT LEFKOWITZ, LATE CHAIRMAN OF THE WIL-
LIAM MORRIS AGENCY IN NEW YORK CITY.

TO ME, YOU WILL ALWAYS REMAIN CLOSE TO MY
HEART FOR YOUR INSPIRATION.

YOU NEVER KNEW IT, BUT YOU WERE ONE OF MY
FAVORITE MENTORS AT THE WILLIAM MORRIS
AGENCY WHEN I TEMPED FOR YOU WHILE MARRIED
TO ONE OF YOUR MOST BRILLIANT, CREATIVE AND
FUNNIEST TELEVISION AGENTS, MICKEY HANFT,
A.K.A. MICKEY McFREE.

THANK YOU FOR BEING THE VISIONARY BUSINESS-
MAN WHO RECOGNIZED MY FUTURE APPROACH TO
"WHOLISM." YOU WERE THE ONLY EXECUTIVE AT
WMA, BESIDES MICKEY, WHO BELIEVED IN ME.

MAY YOUR SOUL REST IN THE PEACEABLE KINGDOM
OF HEAVEN.

I LOVE YOU, MR. LEFKOWITZ.

SPECIAL THANKS TO ALL THOSE PEACE-LOVING PEO-
PLE, PAST, PRESENT (AND FUTURE) WHO INSPIRED
(AND WILL INSPIRE) ME IN THE CREATION OF THIS
BOOK (AND THE FURTHER DEVELOPMENT OF IT) . . .
ESPECIALLY JOANN DAVIS AND MICHELLE SHINSEKI,
FOR THEIR ASSISTANCE, ADVICE AND EDITING.

I WOULD ALSO LIKE TO EXPRESS MY DEEPEST AP-
PRECIATION TO JOANN MCFREE, WHO CREATED THE
PEACE IS CONCEPT IN THIS BOOK. THANK YOU,
SWEET FRIEND.

AND I WILL ALWAYS BE INDEBTED TO DAVID GEF-
FEN'S ENDORSEMENT OF MY "HEARTOONS," HIS
PERSEVERANCE IN TRYING TO GET THEM REPRE-
SENTED BY CAA WHEN MIKE OVITZ SAID NO TO NEW
IMAGES. DON'T FORGET, DAVID, WE HAVE A DATE
ON "MARS."

I ALSO WISH TO THANK KF CHOY, COLLEAGUE AND
SPONSOR OF THE "HEARTOONS" IN THE FAR EAST,
FOR HIS CONTINUED SPIRITUAL SUPPORT.

Lao-tzu wrote:

"A journey of a thousand miles must begin with a single step."

Will you take a single step for peace?

``*I*t isn't enough to talk about
peace.
One must believe in it.
And it isn't enough to believe in it.
One must work for it.''

—Eleanor Roosevelt

"LET US EVERY DAY WORK FOR PEACE WITH OUR MIND AND HEART. EACH OF US SHOULD BEGIN WITH OURSELVES."

—BRIDGE AT REMAGEN PEACE MUSEUM

Introduction

Do you ever get depressed reading the morning paper or watching the evening news? War in the Middle East. Family violence. Suicide. World leaders quarreling over how to make our world a better place. Sometimes a feeling of despair can settle in. The problems seem so large and out of our control. And peace seems elusive.

I used to feel helpless.

Once upon a time, I didn't think that peace would ever settle upon our troubled world. Then I realized that although I am only one person, I am one person and one person can make a difference!

This book is based on my belief that peace on earth begins with you, and me, and each of us. We all must play a part.

This book is designed to provide you with practical tips and suggestions. I hope you find it useful. More important, I hope you are inspired to help create peace.

$\mathscr{P}$EACE BEGINS AT HOME.
IF YOU HAVE A PROBLEM AT HOME,
COMMUNICATE IT. CALL A MEETING
WITH YOUR FAMILY; SIT AROUND THE
KITCHEN TABLE AND DISCUSS
WHAT'S BOTHERING YOU. DON'T BE SHY.
YOU'LL PROBABLY NOT ONLY FIND OUT
THAT EVERYONE WANTS TO HELP
YOU, BUT YOU'LL ALSO
DISCOVER HOW MUCH YOUR
FAMILY LOVES YOU, TOO!

$\mathcal{R}$EMEMBER THAT IT TAKES TWO
TO MAKE AN ARGUMENT.
TURN YOUR CHEEK. REFUSE TO FIGHT.

WORDS CAN DISTURB THE PEACE.
DON'T SPEAK WORDS YOU KNOW WILL
RESULT IN TORMENT.
SPEAK WORDS OF TRUTH THAT WILL
ACCOMPLISH PEACE
AND LOVE IN YOUR LIFE.

*E*LIMINATE TOXIC WORDS.

STUPID. FOOL. IDIOT. LAZY. JERK. BRAT. LOSER. NONE OF THESE WORDS BELONGS IN A PEACEFUL VOCABULARY.

$\mathcal{P}$EACE IS SOMETIMES AN ACT OF
COMPROMISE.
IF YOU ARE AT ODDS WITH SOMEONE,
TRY TO SEE THINGS DIFFERENTLY BY
CHANGING YOUR POINT OF VIEW.
EXPRESS YOURSELF WHENEVER
POSSIBLE, BUT BE FLEXIBLE.

$\mathcal{W}$HAT DO YOU KEEP IN YOUR TOOLBOX
FOR PEACE?

SMILES AND HANDSHAKES COST VERY
LITTLE AND DO MUCH GOOD IN TIMES
OF CONFLICT.

$\mathcal{T}$EDDY ROOSEVELT ONCE WROTE THAT
"TO GOVERN IS TO CHOOSE."

WHAT WILL YOU CHOOSE?

WILL YOU CHOOSE PEACE OR WILL YOU
CHOOSE PAIN?

WHEN PEOPLE HURT YOU,
DON'T STOOP TO THEIR LEVEL.
DO SOMETHING KIND IN RETURN AND
YOU'LL SEE THAT THEY MAY
RESPOND FAVORABLY.

$\mathcal{I}$N ORDER TO ACHIEVE PEACE,
TRY PRACTICING RANDOM ACTS OF
KINDNESS.
AN UNEXPECTED ACT OF LOVE CAN BE
VERY DISARMING.

Be a Peacekeeper . . .

Drop the barriers of fear, mistrust and cynicism. These negative emotions prevent you from the most exquisite joy you will ever know: Peace of Mind.

Peacekeepers

- Sincere apologies
- Pats on the back
- Hugs, handshakes
- Eye contact
- Meeting an opponent halfway
- Win/win philosophy

THE ANGRY SOUL KNOWS NO PEACE.

BREATHE OUT ANGER . . .

BREATHE IN LOVE AND PEACE.

To achieve a feeling of inner peace, meditate once a day. Release the feelings of loneliness, abandonment, despair and alienation . . . all the inner sufferings caused by feelings of hurt and rejection by parents, siblings, spouses and other significant persons.

$\mathscr{I}$F WE DESIRE TO LIVE IN PEACE,
THEN IT IS VERY IMPORTANT TO LISTEN
TO CHILDREN. THEY OFTEN SEE THINGS
MORE INTUITIVELY
THAN ADULTS. IN THEIR INNOCENCE,
CHILDREN CAN BRING MUCH PEACE,
IF WE GIVE THEM A CHANCE.

$\mathcal{D}$O YOU HAVE A BIG HEART?
BIG-HEARTED PEOPLE ACCEPT AND
FORGIVE EVERYONE AND EVERYTHING,
EVEN THOSE WHO HAVE BETRAYED THEM.

THE ACT OF FORGIVENESS
IS ESSENTIAL TO A PEACEFUL MIND.
LET GO OF ANGER AND HOSTILITY.
THEY TAKE AWAY PEACE.

$\mathcal{F}$IND PEACE IN YOURSELF.
IF YOU FEEL ANXIOUS, CLOSE YOUR EYES,
TAKE THREE DEEP BREATHS AND CENTER
YOURSELF. KNOW THAT YOU CAN BE CALM
IN THE MIDST OF STRESS.

$\mathscr{E}$MOTIONAL EXPLOSION LEADS TO SELF-
DESTRUCTION.
TO KEEP THE PEACE, STAY IN CONTROL.

$\mathcal{P}$EACE IS CONTAGIOUS!

MAKE YOUR ENVIRONMENT A PEACEFUL
PLACE AND THEN LET THE PEACE
RADIATE OUT.

$\mathcal{W}$ORDS ARE ENERGY.
POSITIVE WORDS PRODUCE POSITIVE
RESULTS. PEACEFUL WORDS PRODUCE
PEACEFUL RESULTS.

PEACEFUL WORDS:

Good job!
Well done!
You're right!
I agree!
I like it!
I love you!
Thank you!

22

$\mathcal{L}$OVE, DEVOTION AND PEACE ARE
INSEPARABLE.
IF YOU ARE TRULY DEVOTED TO THE ONE
YOU LOVE,
YOU WILL LIVE IN PEACEFUL HARMONY.

$\mathscr{H}$ERE IS A CLUE TO PEACE TO THINK
ABOUT:

WHAT IF THEY GAVE A WAR AND NOBODY
CAME?

$\mathcal{A}$SK FOR GOD'S HELP
IN STRESSFUL SITUATIONS. YOU'LL
BE SURPRISED WHAT CAN HAPPEN
WHEN WE PRAY FOR PEACE.

*I*MAGINE YOUR DREAMS FOR PEACE
COMING TRUE.
DON'T LET THE "DREAM KILLERS" WIN.

DREAM KILLERS

- THE EVENING NEWS
- INTOLERANCE
- NEGATIVE PEOPLE
- WARMONGERS
- INFLEXIBILITY

$\mathcal{V}$ISUALIZE A BANK ACCOUNT
AND FILL IT WITH AFFIRMATIONS OF
PROSPERITY AND PEACE.

AFFIRMATIONS OF PEACE:

- I AM A WINNER.
- I BELIEVE IN WIN/WIN.
- GOD LOVES A PROSPEROUS PERSON.
- IT'S OKAY TO BE PROSPEROUS.
- I AM VALUABLE TO THE WORLD.
- MY CREATIVITY IS HEALTHY.
- I AM COURAGEOUS AND TAKE RISKS.

$\mathcal{W}$HY HOLD A GRUDGE?

DEEP-SEATED RESENTMENTS ONLY BRING
UNHAPPINESS AND DISTURB THE PEACE.

PEACE IS:

*E*XPRESSING YOUR ANGER TOWARD
OTHERS IN HEALTHY WAYS. DON'T ALLOW
ANYONE TO INVADE YOUR BOUNDARIES
WITH ABUSIVE BEHAVIOR.
AND DON'T INVADE THE BOUNDARIES
OF OTHERS WHILE IN CONFLICT.

PEACE IS:

*B*EING NATURAL. YOU DON'T HAVE TO
ANALYZE EVERYTHING YOU DO AND
EVERYTHING YOU SAY.

SOLVE PROBLEMS.
DON'T DISSECT THEM!

$\mathscr{P}$UT YOUR HURT ASIDE.

PEACE
IS LOOKING SOMEONE IN THE
EYE AND TELLING THEM THAT
YOU LOVE THEM.

$\mathcal{P}$EACE IS:
RESPECTING YOURSELF. WHEN YOU
RESPECT YOURSELF, YOU WILL LOOK AT
OTHERS DIFFERENTLY.

$\mathcal{C}$URSING AND SWEARING DISTURB THE
PEACE. SOMEONE MAY GET SERIOUSLY
HURT BY RASH WORDS, AND YOU'LL
NEVER FIND PEACE OF MIND.

THE WORLD IS CHANGING RAPIDLY.
NOW IS THE TIME TO WORK ON YOUR EGO
AND JOIN THE PEACEMAKERS OF THE UNI-
VERSE. REMEMBER, DINOSAURS ARE
ONLY VALUABLE IN MUSEUMS AND FILMS.

PEACE IS:

Curbing your emotional outbursts. Violent emotions, such as rage and jealousy, often lead to painful regrets.

"I HATE YOU!"

HOW MANY TIMES HAVE YOU HURT
THE HEART OF ANOTHER WITH THESE
WORDS?

*H*AVE YOU EVER GONE OUT OF
YOUR WAY FOR SOMEONE OTHER THAN
YOURSELF?

WHAT ARE YOU WAITING FOR?

$\mathcal{R}$ELEASING HATRED FROM YOUR HEART
WILL REWARD YOU WITH A PEACEFUL
MIND.

$\mathcal{M}$USIC CAN BE SOOTHING AND VERY PEACEFUL. TRY LISTENING TO YOUR FAVORITE MUSIC TO BRING ABOUT CALM. ENJOY THE MOMENT.

$\mathcal{P}$RAY. PAINT. BE SILENT
AND HEAR THE INVISIBLE INTELLIGENCE
OF THE UNIVERSE CALLING OUT FOR
PEACE.

CAN YOU HEAR IT?

$\mathcal{A}$LBERT EINSTEIN ONCE SAID,
"PEACE CANNOT BE KEPT BY FORCE.
IT CAN ONLY BE ACHIEVED BY
UNDERSTANDING."

WILL YOU MAKE AN EFFORT TO
UNDERSTAND?

PEACE IS:

$\mathscr{F}$INDING THE POSITIVE IN A NEGATIVE
SITUATION AND TURNING IT AROUND.
CREATE HUMOR AND DON'T TAKE
YOURSELF SO SERIOUSLY.

PEACE IS:

$\mathcal{K}$NOWING THAT YOU ARE IN PERFECT
HARMONY WITH THE UNIVERSE WHEN YOU
THINK IN AN AFFIRMATIVE WAY.

$\mathcal{B}$LESSED ARE THE PEACEMAKERS,
FOR THEY SHALL BE CALLED THE
CHILDREN OF GOD.

$\mathcal{A}$VOID WORDS, LABELS AND EXPRESSIONS, WHENEVER POSSIBLE, THAT DISTURB THE PEACE, SUCH AS

> STUPID
> YOU NO GOOD B@#*!!—YOU ARE A
>   LOSER!
> SLOB
> DUMMY
> YOU'RE JUST LIKE YOUR DUMB FATHER.
> YOU'RE GOING TO GROW UP BEING A
>   NOBODY.

THESE NEGATIVE WORDS DESTROY AND DIVIDE PEOPLE.
WHY NOT EMBRACE WORDS THAT BRING PEACE? HERE ARE SOME EXPRESSIONS:

> YOU'RE FABULOUS!
> WHAT AN ANGEL!
> LOVABLE
> YOU'RE SO KIND.
> YOU'RE SO SENSITIVE.
> THAT'S TERRIFIC.
> I FORGIVE YOU.

45

*T*HIS IS A VERY PEACEFUL GALLERY TO VISIT IF YOU'RE EVER IN HONG KONG:

PLUM BLOSSOMS
17/F CODA PLAZA
51 GARDEN ROAD
CENTRAL
HONG KONG

WHY NOT CREATE A PEACEFUL GALLERY CLOSE TO YOUR HOME?

$\mathcal{D}$ID YOU KNOW THAT THERE ARE FIFTY PEACE MUSEUMS AROUND THE WORLD? WHY NOT MAKE ONE OF THE MUSEUMS A THEME FOR YOUR NEXT VACATION? HERE'S A SUGGESTION:

NOBEL PEACE PRIZE MUSEUM
C/O NORWEGIAN NOBEL INSTITUTE
DRAMMENSVEIEN 19
N-0255 OSLO
NORWAY

$\mathcal{S}$TEER YOURSELF TOWARD PEACE.
GRAVITATE TOWARD PEACEFUL PEOPLE,
PLACES AND SITUATIONS.

$\mathcal{C}$REATE A PEACE LIBRARY.

READ WORKS BY THE PEACEMAKERS:

LAO-TZU
ABE LINCOLN
GANDHI
MOSES
BUDDHA
MARTIN LUTHER KING, JR.

$\mathcal{F}$ORM AND JOIN COMMUNITIES OF
PEACE.

JOIN THE PEACE CORPS.
BECOME A PEACE FREAK.
CREATE A PEACE MARCH.
UNITE PEACEMONGERS.
LINK PEACE LOVERS TOGETHER.

$\mathcal{G}$OD'S PEACE.

CAN YOU FEEL IT?

$\mathcal{P}$EACE FOR SALE.

SURPRISE! IT'S FREE!!

$\mathcal{T}$o err is human, to forgive,

divine. . . .

``WHEN THE MOON
IS IN THE SEVENTH HOUSE
AND JUPITER ALIGNS WITH MARS
THEN PEACE WILL GUIDE THE PLANETS
AND LOVE WILL STEER THE STARS
THIS IS THE DAWNING OF
THE AGE OF AQUARIUS.
THE AGE OF AQUARIUS . . .''
—FROM *HAIR* (1966)

$\mathcal{M}$Y DEAR FRIEND BOB DYLAN,
A PEACEMAKER, WROTE "THE TIMES THEY
ARE A-CHANGIN' " IN THE SIXTIES.

I AGREE:
THE TIMES THEY *ARE*
A-CHANGIN', AND WE
CAN ALL PLAY A PART IN
MAKING THIS A MORE
PEACEFUL WORLD.
"DON'T BE A PEACE LOSER!"

$\mathcal{L}$ISTEN CAREFULLY
TO JOHN LENNON'S SONG
"GIVE PEACE A CHANCE"

. . . AND THEN REALLY GIVE PEACE A
CHANCE!

$\mathcal{N}$EWS BULLETIN FROM A
PEACEMAKER . . .

"THE METROPOLITAN PEACE MUSEUM OF
NEW YORK WILL LINK THE INTERNA-
TIONAL NETWORK OF PEACE MUSEUMS TO
THE UNITED NATIONS, CREATING A
WORLDWIDE WEB OF PEACE AND CREATIV-
ITY IN THE TWENTY-FIRST CENTURY."

—SANDY HINDEN, EXECUTIVE DIRECTOR
METROPOLITAN PEACE MUSEUM

$\mathcal{E}$LDRIDGE CLEAVER ONCE WROTE,
"YOU'RE EITHER PART OF THE SOLUTION
OR PART OF THE PROBLEM."

JOIN US AND BE PART OF THE PEACE
SOLUTION!

58

$\mathscr{A}$LWAYS BEAR IN MIND
THAT EACH OF US IS ENTITLED TO
LIFE, LIBERTY AND THE PURSUIT OF
INNER PEACE!

PEACE IS:

Going camping in the woods
alone and enjoying nature. Meditate
and visualize
How great it is to be alive.

*N*URTURE YOUR CHILDREN.
DON'T CRIPPLE THEM EMOTIONALLY WITH
WORDS THAT DISABLE. THESE COMMENTS
DURING A FAMILY CONFLICT WILL CAUSE
ONLY HURT AND, PERHAPS, IRREPARABLE
DAMAGE.

AVOID DESTRUCTIVE EXPRESSIONS
SUCH AS

"DUMMY—YOU'VE GOT NO BRAINS!"
"NO, YOU CAN'T DO THAT BECAUSE
YOU'RE HANDICAPPED."

$\mathcal{F}$ROM THE GOSPEL OF ST. THOMAS: "IF YOU BRING FORTH THAT WHICH IS WITHIN YOU, IT WILL SAVE YOU. IF YOU DO NOT BRING FORTH THAT WHICH IS WITHIN YOU, IT WILL DESTROY YOU."

$\mathcal{E}$VERY DAY THE WORLD CHANGES, BRINGING NEW THREATS AND/OR NEW HOPE. WHAT VIBRATION ARE YOU TAPPING INTO? TAP INTO PEACE.

*A*NGER-HURT-SHAME-GUILT-
TRAUMA . . .
WHICH ONE KEEPS YOU FROM ATTAINING
A PEACEFUL MIND-SET?

$\mathcal{M}$ORE CLUES TO PEACE . . .
DISCOVER WAYS TO FEEL LIKE A WINNER
RATHER THAN BEING OBSESSED WITH
DEFEAT.

"Nothing will bring you more happiness and peace of mind than getting lean, strong and healthy. Start eating higher volume . . . higher quality foods."

—*STOP THE INSANITY!* SUSAN POWTER

$\mathcal{L}$ET'S HAVE A RACE.

THE GOAL IS A PEACEFUL MIND.

GET READY . . . SET . . .

ON YOUR MARK . . .

GO PEACE!

$\mathcal{T}$RY BEING THE PIED PIPER OF PEACE.

IF YOU CAN'T PLAY THE FLUTE, TRY
WHISTLING.

$\mathcal{M}$Y MOTHER FOUND A GREAT DEAL OF
PEACE CULTIVATING A GARDEN AND SHE
LOVED PLANTING COLORFUL FLOWERS,
TOO. PLANT A PEACEFUL GARDEN.

$\mathcal{P}$EACE, LIKE LIFE, MUST BEGIN AT
HOME.

``A MUSICIAN MUST MAKE MUSIC,
AN ARTIST MUST PAINT,
A POET MUST WRITE,
IF HE IS TO BE ULTIMATELY AT PEACE
WITH HIMSELF.
WHAT A MAN CAN BE, HE MUST BE.''

—ABRAHAM H. MASLOW

PEACE IS:

*K*NOWING THAT A BROKEN HEART
IS JUST A STEPPING-STONE TO YOUR TRUE
LOVE.

—MARY ANN ASMAR

$\mathcal{T}$HE CHALLENGE OF THE NEXT
CENTURY IS TO BUILD A BRIDGE TO
PEACEFUL LIVING.

"You have to take chances for peace . . . the ability to get to the verge without getting into the war is the necessary art. If you try to run away from it, if you are scared to go to the brink . . . you are lost!"

—James Shepley, author, 1956

CAN YOU THINK OF TEN REASONS WHY
SOME PEOPLE CAN'T FIND PEACE OF
MIND?

CAN YOU THINK OF ONE REASON WHY
YOU CAN'T?

``*F*irst keep the peace within
yourself
Then you can also bring peace to
others.''

—Jan Huss, 1372–1415
(last words at the stake)

$\mathcal{P}$EACE ON EARTH BEGINS WITH YOU!

"THERE CAN BE NO PROGRESS
(REAL, THAT IS, MORAL)
EXCEPT IN THE INDIVIDUAL AND BY THE
INDIVIDUAL, HIMSELF."

—CHARLES BAUDELAIRE

PEACE IS:

*K*NOWING HOW TO USE
YOUR POWERS OF THOUGHT, IMAGINATION
AND INTUITION TO NAVIGATE DURING
THE TRANSFORMATIONAL TIMES
OF THE NEW MILLENNIUM.

PEACE IS:

$\mathcal{K}$NOWING HOW TO TRANSFORM
LIMITING, SELF-DESTRUCTIVE ATTITUDES
AND EMOTIONS INTO THE BUILDING
BLOCKS OF A PURPOSEFUL, JOY-FILLED
LIFE.

$\mathscr{P}$EACEFUL REFLECTIONS BRING

PEACEFULNESS.

"*M*AN IS SOMETIMES
EXTRAORDINARILY
PASSIONATELY IN LOVE WITH
SUFFERING."

—FYODOR DOSTOEVSKY

WHY NOT BE IN LOVE WITH PEACE?

``*I* AM ONLY ONE,
BUT STILL I AM ONE.
I CANNOT DO EVERYTHING,
but still I CAN DO SOMETHING,
AND BECAUSE I CANNOT DO EVERYTHING
I WILL NOT REFUSE TO DO THE SOME-
THING THAT I CAN DO.''

—EDWARD E. HALE, 1822–1909

LEND A HAND TO PEACE

``AND IF EVER I TOUCHED A LIFE I
HOPE THAT LIFE KNOWS
THAT I KNOW THAT TOUCHING WAS AND
STILL IS AND ALWAYS WILL BE THE TRUE
REVOLUTION''

—NIKKI GIOVANNI

TOUCH A LIFE WITH PEACE . . .

"To everything there is a season, and a
time to every purpose under the heaven:
A time to be born, and a time to die;
A time to plant, and a time to
pluck up that which is planted;
A time to kill, and a time to heal;
A time to break down, and a time to
build up;
A time to weep, and a time to laugh;
A time to mourn, and a time to dance;
A time to cast away stones,
and a time to gather stones together;
A time to embrace, and a time to re-
frain from embracing;
A time to get, and a time to lose; a
time to keep, and a time to cast away;
A time to rend, and a time to sew; a
time to keep silence, and a time to speak;
A time to love, and a time to hate;
A time of war, and a time of PEACE."

—Ecclesiastes

Let Now Be a Time of Peace!

$\mathcal{R}$EST IN PEACE? LIVE IN PEACE!

DON'T MAKE IT YOUR GOAL TO HAVE
PEACE ONLY IN THE AFTERLIFE. MAKE IT
YOUR GOAL TO HAVE PEACE THROUGHOUT
LIFE.

$\mathcal{T}$HE TIME FOR PEACE IS NOW.

DON'T PUT IT OFF.

DON'T START TOMORROW.

DON'T BE AFRAID TO TRY.

NOW IS THE TIME TO SPREAD SOME

PEACE.

Proactive, not Reactive!

You have the power to change the world. You don't have to depend on the government, or the system, or your parents, or your teachers. It's all you—exciting, isn't it?

CREATE A PEACE WALL.

COLLECT SAYINGS, ART AND PICTURES
DEVOTED TO PEACE AND PUT THEM ABOVE
YOUR DESK. MAKE YOUR POINT OF
REFERENCE A PEACEFUL ONE.

Develop peaceful habits.
Habits become second nature.
Peace can become a natural
part of your life.

"Go PLACIDLY AMID THE NOISE
AND HASTE AND REMEMBER WHAT
PEACE THERE MAY BE IN SILENCE . . .

"BE AT PEACE WITH GOD,
WHATEVER YOU CONCEIVE HIM TO BE
AND WHATEVER YOUR LABORS AND
ASPIRATIONS
IN THE NOISY CONFUSION OF LIFE,
KEEP PEACE WITH YOUR SOUL."

—DESIDERATA, 1692

``$\mathscr{T}$HERE NEVER WAS A GOOD WAR, OR A
BAD PEACE.''

—BENJAMIN FRANKLIN

``The Lord bless you, and keep
you:
The Lord make His face to shine
upon you,
and be gracious unto you:
The Lord lift up His countenance
upon you,
and give you PEACE!''

—Numbers 6:24–26

``PEACE IS JUST A FIVE-LETTER WORD:

P EOPLE

E NTHUSIASTICALLY

A CTING

C IVILLY

E VERY DAY!''

—JOANN MCFREE

$\mathcal{I}$N ORDER TO ACHIEVE SOMETHING,
WE MUST FEEL WE DESERVE IT.
WE DESERVE PEACE!

—MICKEY MCFREE
EXECUTIVE PRODUCER OF DOCUMENTARY
THE HISTORY OF THE HEARTOONS
(WORK-IN-PROGRESS)

``PEACE IS:

LIKING YOURSELF

PEACE IS:

HAVING SELF-ESTEEM

PEACE IS:

THE ABSENCE OF FEAR

PEACE IS:

KNOWING YOU'VE DONE YOUR BEST.''

—JOANN MCFREE

ART DIRECTOR OF DOCUMENTARY

THE HISTORY OF THE HEARTOONS

(WORK-IN-PROGRESS)

"A Recipe for Peace:
Mix equal parts of kindness, forgive-
ness and trust.
Serve with a warm heart."

—Joann McFree
art director of documentary
THE HISTORY OF THE HEARTOONS
(work-in-progress)

"THE TAO IS THE ETERNAL WAY.
IT IS SOUND ADVICE TO THE HUMAN SOUL
NOT TO TAKE THINGS INTO EXTREMES.
IT IS A CALL FOR INNER STRENGTH
TO DWELL IN TRANQUILLITY
AND PEACE OF MIND."

—KF CHOY, BUSINESSMAN

''WAR IS NOT HEALTHY FOR CHILDREN AND OTHER LIVING THINGS.''

—SISTER CORITA

"ARMS ALONE ARE NOT ENOUGH
TO KEEP THE PEACE.
IT MUST BE KEPT BY MEN."

—JFK

ARE WE MEN AND WOMEN ENOUGH TO
KEEP THE PEACE?

FARIDI MCFREE IS THE FOUNDER OF THE STUDIO OF THE HEALING HEARTS IN NEW YORK CITY. SHE IS A SPIRITUAL ARTIST, COUNSELOR, WRITER AND LECTURER IN THE FIELD OF SELF-HEALING THROUGH CREATIVITY.

THE STUDIO OF THE HEALING HEARTS (SHH) WISHES TO OPEN THE DOOR TO A MAJOR LEAP IN EVOLUTION. OUR DREAM IS TO CREATE A TV SERIES OF DOCUMENTARY FILMS THAT WOULD BE INTERACTIVE SO THAT THE PIONEERS OF PEACE AND LOVE AND EVERYONE WHO IS HELPING TO CHANGE THE CONSCIOUSNESS OF THE PLANET CAN SHARE THEIR STORIES. IF WE PUT OUR MINDS AND HEARTS TOGETHER, WE CAN AFFECT EVERYTHING!

WE'RE INTERACTIVE, SO STAY "TOONED-IN" FOR OUR UP-AND-COMING TREASURE HUNT FOR PEACE. OUR AIM IS TO WIN THE NOBEL PEACE PRIZE! WE HOPE YOU'LL JOIN US, TOO.

IF YOU WISH TO CONTACT THE STUDIO, PLEASE WRITE TO
THE STUDIO OF THE HEALING HEARTS
355 SOUTH END AVENUE
NEW YORK, NEW YORK 10280–1010